To my beautiful wife Kimsy,

I love you more than all the words

I could ever write.

Contents

Intro

Being normal

I had moments (years of them actually) when I had convinced myself that I couldn't carry on, that I was crazy, and I was a burden to those around me. I wrongly blamed myself for things in my past which then controlled my thoughts and my future. Lows of utter despair and fear almost consumed me. I felt like I was alone with no hope of ever getting back to being 'normal'.

I'm not normal, far from it, but who is? What I mean by being normal, is to be free from the chains of anxiety and worry caused by irrational thoughts and stress. That would be my normal. Maybe you can relate with similar feelings?

Expressing honest emotions in poetry is not really 'normal' or something society expects from a bloke. But I'm not a normal bloke, I'm a 47-year-old boy who still does wheelies. I honestly don't care if people judge me, I've never been one to abide by the never-ending High School rules of social acceptance. Always original, never ashamed is my party line. I do what I want and am never embarrassed by what I wear, write, do or say. Writing helps me think rationally, it makes me understand and trust/decide how to feel normal.

Overthinking, stress, sleepless nights and anxiety were just some of my anti-superpowers! They literally crippled my mind, body and soul for years, and I think I hid them really well from almost everyone. I was ashamed of my mental weakness and the 'mard arse' stigma it carried.

Yet without my anti-superpowers I suppose I would have never discovered what was going on around me and what life was all about. I've learnt so much about who I am and the cause of my controlling fears. My experiences of coming back from the edge of insanity and my love for life are shared in the poems I write.

After I first shared my poems on social media I received lots of amazing inbox messages from friends/strangers offering their love and support. I also received lots of messages empathising with my quarry from people experiencing tough times themselves. I've seen a whole new side of people who I've known for years, a side I would have never known existed if I hadn't shared my own years of despair/self-discovery.

My honesty has given me the freedom to live an open life, hopefully my experiences of darker days will help others see light. Help realise that those inner voices and thoughts are not in control but will make you a better person the more you understand what's going on.

I now see my darker days were a sort of blessing, they were something I had to endure in order to become the person I am today. That person is here to listen and help as many people as I can. I think that's what I'm here for, it's what I'm meant to do. I'm not saying I'm a modern-day Jesus or owt (even though I am a skilled carpenter), I just want people to be happy and enjoy life.

Over time I've found that a divine love/damaged mind can generate many a word; I'm a poet by circumstance.

From the first moment we kissed

You share in my sunshine,
construed as indelible etchings
in this timeline.

My pensive thoughts all revealing,
a book of torn pages
defined by our meaning.

Incandescent fervor for the life we make,
being the best for each other
from each moment we wake.

A bond unique, of pure devotion,
truly thicker than blood,
superfluous from absolution.

To be loved is to be missed,
I knew it was special
from the first moment we kissed.

Tenacious propensity of avid amour,
beyond simple attraction;
a love so beautiful, to outlast ever more.

Always hoping for that tomorrow

When our own solitude
is found in things we write,

when our inept rationale
keeps us awake all through the night.

From barred windows of conjecture
confusion amplifies frustration,

clinging to our sanity
is not a lucid exaggeration.

An abyss of torrid thoughts
overwhelming weight upon our shoulders,

a hollow emptiness inside
in desperation for someone to hold us.

Detached from all normality
a sordid numbness of sense,

lost and alone
seemingly beyond any recompense.

Our brave face, a mere front
a public show of fiction,

a crass disguise of white deceit
to conceal our mental affliction.

Void of any cohesion
without a path to follow,

we try to smile on the outside
and hope for a better day tomorrow.

Loves back wheel

Never did I ever
dream about being forty-seven,
especially when I feel I'm still in my teens.

Creaking knees, lungs that wheeze
a medical marvel,
rattling with vitamins and pills.

Tiring days that fade
off up early to bed,
for nights of very little sleep.

As I glimpse towards my own frailty,
knowing I will never be that boy again is bewildering,
yet inside I will always be him.

An ageing dad who's still rad
and loves back wheel.
My life lived with a smile, as if one endless wheelie.

It was never my fault

Void of compassion for the ones who had let me down,
my true nature deferred
as post-traumatic stress influenced my future.

A disconsolate road I endured in silence,
as I walked a path of shameful uncertainty
desperately trying not to reveal my weakness.

I somehow then managed to lose myself,
completely engulfed by anxiety
in the worry of losing others.

I really struggled to find a way back,
deluded by the panic
of drowning in the depths of my own irrational thoughts.

An intoxicating loneliness,
of misleading remorse
distracting from a life I really needed to be living.

Yet I somehow managed to forge my own way,
to find my own meaning
recapture my focus and trust the best of me to shine through.

An arduous journey, of self-blame and discovery
mentally scarring, but ultimately having the resilience to believe;
those bad times are forgotten and will not define who I really am.

So, as I stand in my own truth
I am no longer consumed by despair
I see opportunity, love and laughter, I'm me again.

Things I've learned

As sure as is the sky is blue,
Mr. Benn was a transvestite on glue.

That Time is the most corrosive force
and Time will always run its course.

Ignorant passengers raise their voices
love and hate are not the only choices.

Nonchalant fools of self-importance
rape the world beyond its sustenance.

A race so capable of amazing feats
yet we cast our rubbish into oceans and streets.

Frivolous, careless, wastefully outrageous
traits of character which so often betray us.

Bemused by religions, wars and past glory
frustrated I can't predict the end of my story.

Angered by things I can't control
allowing faults of others to burden my soul.

We break, we cry, we laugh, we heal
peril and magic are part of the deal.

Hypocrisy is rife within our society
drunk on life I lecture on sobriety.

Stars they sparkle, flowers bloom
a single smile lights up a room.

Belly laughs and squashy cuddles
rescue me from gloomy puddles.

Highs and lows of life all revealing
love is the most incredible feeling.

Wonders of nature flank my progression
a life gifted from chaos, is such a fascinating lesson.

Just what have we become

The world turns and life goes on,
manifesting from beautiful watercolour
to smudged black ink,
as our species rapes the world, we take for granted.

A world of uncertainty
of ignorance, of anger,
a world of hatred,
of hypocrisy and danger.

A world of the self-righteous
of ignorance, of racism
a world of disrespect, of fake news
and fascism.

A world of contempt
of extremism, of greed,
a world of outrage, of killing
and materialistic need.

Where footballers/pop stars are sensationalised as genius
paid millions and devoutly idolised,
where in truth a genius is a single mother/father raising a child,
or nurse/doctor/emergency service simply saving lives.

Lacking compassion,
bereft of fun,
our presence on this world is embarrassing;
just what have we become.

Unforgivable

A convergence of self-preservation
of rationale and realisation.

The hatred I had for that alter ego
a distain contempt that only I know.

Every day I never miss you
erasing memories because I need to.

Overthinking woes betrayed me
hopelessness and worry nearly drove me crazy.

All the things you put me through
let it be known that I've disowned you.

No longer are you part of my path
even before your demise I never looked back.

The truth is I don't owe you
you broke my heart now I no longer know you.

I had the courage to move on
it took a long time, but those struggles are now gone.

I've learned a lot from them
how to be strong and how to love again.

Your selfishness beyond recompense
deplorable actions that never made any sense.

The pain was both mental and physical
and despite who you were to me, you are simply unforgivable.

Moments of our love

Blue skies mottled by
plumes of cotton dreams,

golden rays come searing through
crepuscular angel beams.

Tired leaves spiral down
a breeze whispers them away,

burning glow atop the trees
defines a perfect autumn day.

Sheer brilliance of the golden hour
enhancing beauty all around,

hasty creatures seek retreat
their shadows so profound.

Hot drinks and rosy cheeks
by a crackling open fire,

wishing on the stars with you
is my heart's desire.

Holding on wrapped tight together
as the moonlight gleams,

happy to our hearts content
as if fuelled by our dreams.

Cosy warm infectious cuddles
compelling smiles and laughter,

moments of our love shine through
to be remembered forever after.

Killing fields

Riding through the countryside
is so beautiful.
The rolling hills
and views are incredible.

Until I pass by the fields of death;
the 'live' stock seemingly waiting to die,
their short lives spent mercilessly unloved
their eyes forlorn as if they want to cry.

Young lambs and calves
dragged bleating from their mothers,
confused and scared
to the abattoir with the others.

Amid cries of pain
and stench of fear,
poor terrified animals
give out their last tear.

Burgers, joints,
shanks, steak,
murdered souls
served on a plate.

To save them all
to roam and be free,
to be with their herds
to live full lives and be happy.

In a world of eat or be eaten,
I'm just an empathetic fool,
who despises natural selection
and wonders why life has to be so cruel.

Marginal Tourists

Life, is what your dreams
are supposed to be.
Do them today,
those things you've always wanted to do.
Feel the rush,
of what your imagination would only see.

Dare to enjoy,
to seek fulfilment without excuse.
Be yourself,
be free to live how you want to live.
Distance yourself,
from the procrastination recluse.

Be your bucket list,
don't be content with just having one.
You've only one chance,
fill up your time with experiences.
No one will remember you,
for being cautious when your gone.

We make our own choices,
without pathways to define.
Be different,
have faith in your own virtues.
We are but brief visitors,
as marginal tourists in time.

Fighting tears we will smile.

In spite
of the inevitability of life
we carry on,

with disregard
for this façade
we mourn those who've gone.

Consoled
by the ones left to hold
we can only ask why,

why us again
why not them
we cannot comprehend but we try.

Destined from the start
for family to be torn apart
we pretend that we are fine,

the chaos of fate
an unknown date
eventually betrayed by unforgiving time.

No chance to redact
it's how we react
once we have all cried,

our heads held high
we will always defy
that sickening emptiness inside.

We will smile and take pleasure
remembering times we had together
how we all laughed and played,

as our guide you are instilled
making you proud as we rebuild
we can only hope the sadness will fade;
 - but you and your smile will never be forgotten.

Our love, immortal

A glint in the shadows
your guiding light
through darkest times
illuminating your path,

forged together
bound by a promise
to love to cherish
to live and to laugh.

Tireless fortitude
defined togetherness
existing as one
an eternal fire,

our hearts entwined
into submission
unrivalled passion
unrelenting desire.

When you scatter my soul
amongst the stars
I'll watch over you
as you count the days,

unperturbed
by the fabric of time
our love immortal
forever and always.

Extinction Rebellion

The callous walk among us
materialistic whores forever greedy,
shaming the beleaguered
ignoring desperation of the needy.

Inculpable to moral responsibility
without thought without due care,
a delusional complacency
for the dying planet that we share.

Simple minded in destruction
of which there's no defense,
as we procrastinate, the wrath of nature
will reveal our consequence.

The power of the people
challenging the self-righteous elite,
eroding absolutist corruption
for demands we will make them meet.

Not just words or self-privilege
a genuine force of proud distinction,
as a certain rebellion gains momentum
against our very own extinction.

The chaotic school of life.

Reluctant living
life is sometimes so unforgiving,
yet together we will share in the adversity.

Loss is inevitable
yet always uncomfortable,
it's how we cope that will inevitably define us.

Categorising tears
compartmentalising fears,
emotionally sceptic toward cognitive malfunction.

Intermittent happiness
is not a measure of our success,
love, compassion and empathy our only guides.

Despite society's voices
there are no correct choices,
we must choose a path to what we think is right.

Without ethnic identity
nor religious unity,
we are honest people simply trying to survive.

Our best we give
on the journey we live,
but we won't ever claim to be perfect.

The world we embrace
as our love radiates,
perpetually evolving in the chaotic school of life.

Be your best

Time
is the most valuable thing I have
I spend it wisely,

love
is my favourite gift to give
I share it precisely.

Kindness
is a strength I show profusely
it's free to all,

empathy
is something which can devour me
or simply not at all.

Forgiveness
when betrayed is not my best trait
I'm not to blame,

my smile
is as honest as my words
I expect the same.

Dedication
my heart belongs to very few
in them I trust,

ambition
I seek to achieve my dreams
because I must.

Inspiration
I strive to offer in abundance
without rest,

life
the greatest gift bestowed upon us;
just try to be your best.

Time won't wait, for you to be you

Are you alive or just living?
Maybe looking for a new beginning,
to prove to yourself
that you actually matter.

From behind a broken smile
you've known that for a while,
the loneliness inside
is trying to take over.

Forget what you've learned
give up all that you've earned,
and slump gracefully down
into your disconsolate rut.

Awash with egregious guilt
leaving all that you've built,
you surrender your life
through a fallen mind of disparity.

Is that you defeated?
Feeling like you've been cheated,
tricked into submission
slowly dying in your dreams.

Ask yourself, are you alive or just living?
Go grab that new beginning,
prove to yourself
that you do actually matter.

No doubt everyone is alone
in this very temporary home,
because although we are together
we are all, simply orphans of time.

Our insignificance

Unbearably slow
yet uncontrollably fast
an invisible force
dilutes presence into past.

Mere specs through time
offering feeble resistance
as insignificant others
despite our self-important existence.

A combination of atoms
an evolutionary prowess
gifted the status of life
from chaotic redress.

Our irrelevant dots
scour endlessly for reverence
among trillions of light years
we seek out our own relevance.

In the grand scheme of things
our two minutes of glory
are the most paltry of lines
in a much bigger story.

An infinitely vast universe
perhaps one unexplainable entity
in a place of pure wonder;
when, where and what are we...?

Love is everything

I dream about a mental cage
the one I wish I could escape
trapped inside a fragile mind
wired profusely like a Pollock painting,

delinquent ghosts of cynicism
linger around inside my head
a reluctant puppet to constant anguish
imprisoned by such tainting.

Conceived unto forlorn despair
gripped by unforgiving torment
lost amid unrepentant terror
frightened into self-induced seclusion,

a battle rages to regain control
struggling incessantly to find a way
to breath, to live, to be like all the others
my thoughts waylaid by irrational delusion.

Brief moments of hope
flicker faintly through fears
as I remember my tired mind
is no place for an afflicted imagination,

cast far adrift from normality
upon a cloud of invisible misery
with little belief it could ever end;
yet I know that love, can be my only salvation.

Melancholy fools

a mood to dim the brightest star
to question who you really are.

Self-demising thoughts of foul
eclipse and shroud an anguished soul.

Floods of fears drown rationale
as if devoured by mental femme fatale.

The weak they yield, ground to succumb
plied with drugs prescribed to numb.

Of all the things, we take for granted given
the chance of life should keep us driven.

Desires and loved ones pass us by
time devours all in the blink of an eye.

A pinch of stoicism mixed with hope
exorcise those tainted thoughts of mope.

Be grateful for the simple things
enjoy the challenges that your life brings.

Pits of empathy manifest concern
caring too much, a harsh lesson to learn.

Rejoice the day to live each moment
find your balance between delight and torment.

Precious times they fuel our quarry
making us simple fools of melancholy.

.
;

A fake smile
an injured soul
lost inside the darkest hole.

Forlorn regress
invisible pain
trapped beneath an endless rain.

Choked by thoughts
controlled by fear
convincing that the end is near.

Vitality drained
impoverished dreams
life force seeps from creaking seams.

Defeated demeanor
without redress
consumed by uncontrollable stress.

Running scared
alone inside
nowhere rational left to hide.

A glint of light
you hear someone say,
it's ok to be not ok.

Epiphany strikes
realisation ensues
your mind is yours, it's yours to lose.

An unconditional unity

Head over heels
on one of my wheels,
I'm in love with you, I always will be.

Eclectic amour
if I could possibly love you more,
you know that I would.

Definitively yours
my life has one cause,
I'm encompassed in you.

An unconditional unity
since the inevitable opportunity,
from when our paths crossed.

Our lives entwined
as our memories remind,
how far we've come together.

Understandably devoted
our passion duly noted,
as we seek our dream by the sea.

Hand in hand
by sea and sand,
we can start a new adventure.

Turning back years
of perverse oscillation,
reliving the memories
fouled by time's degradation.

Backtracking to moments
once shared with a lost one,
consumed in euphoria
at a chance to have held them.

Seeds of entitlement torment
flourish relentlessly to bloom,
once vast plains of time
evaporate soullessly into doom.

A reluctant observer
to desperation and glory,
to witness the journeys of others
and to share in their story.

Slipping in between chaos
of historical days,
navigating cruel shadows
and the relative pathways.

Without confrontational paradox
or disrupted timelines,
resisting temptation to embellish
even the most cherished of lives.

A dimensional passenger
or trustee of time,
a chrononaut's adventure
not to your own design.

Epoch nonchalance
with putrid resistance,
eclipsed by the solipsism,
of your very own existence.

On our journey through time

Every time I see you smile,
I feel like I'm the luckiest man in the world.

All the times I've made you smile,
are just my dreams coming true.

As I sit and stare off into the distance,
thoughts of you, make me fuzzy inside.

Your scent, your taste, your habitual quirks,
keep me focused when I need you the most.

But I can never miss you, you're always a part of me,
together we are one, on our journey through time.

A modern-day Guy Fawkes required

The people's choice?
The majority's voice?
Were all the votes counted?

First past the post,
or the side who had the most?
A tainted ballot none the less.

Has far right won?
Is democracy undone?
Coerced by a house of greedy liars!

For or agin' ?
Better out or better in?
But who can we believe?

Second agendas of deceit,
they try to take the seat,
while embarrassing our great nation.

Unkept promises of reward,
turning on allies from abroad,
a referendum without sanity.

A deal so far away,
a Parliament in disarray,
only a Guy Fawkes can save us.

Labelled

From fractured reality
evolves transient existence,
an invisible consequence
despite all my resistance.

A mind so lost
yet without despair,
detached from the world
seemingly beyond repair.

A metaphorical bubble
of procrastination,
overthinking woes
spawn anxious anticipation.

Candescent remorse
self-blaming duress,
time slips by unnoticed
during philosophical regress.

Claustrophobic neurosis
a solitude of stillness,
an aberration of normality
simply labelled, mental illness.

Always original

I really didn't know
how to survive,
until it all made sense
in my mind tonight.

I don't look back,
I believe my choices,
ignoring destructive advice
from pensive voices.

I try to laugh
find time to smile,
seek happiness in anything
if only for a while.

Learn from my experiences
never smothered by feelings,
trusting myself to live
to define my own meanings.

I do things I love
without any regret,
I don't know my limits
I've not found them yet.

I share my compassion
without burdening guilt,
gaining strength from achievements
and all that I've built.

I am my own person
not one to be tamed,
I'm always original
and never ashamed.

On trial

Shrouded in darkness
living off memories
thrown out like tired old shoes,

forgotten by many
blending into the background
feeling like yesterday's news.

Perplexed by time
with no one to turn to
a loneliness so painful and enduring,

constrained to the shadows
cast by melancholy silhouettes
realising the seclusion they bring.

Mentally trapped
imprisoned by thoughts
bemoaning the ability to smile,

unable to break free
to disengage from the torment
of a life living constantly on trial.

Neil

Always smiling,
always laughing.
An example to others,
of happiness, of strength, and sheer determination.

Modest, unassuming,
trusting and truthful.
Take pride in his friendship,
and the memories you shared.

Courageous, hardworking,
reliable and honest.
A unique kindness,
that knew no bounds.

An abundance of energy,
fuelled his thirst for adventure.
On land or in water,
Neil forged his own way.

A friend, a colleague,
a teacher and trainer.
A loving son and brother,
who gave everything he could.

An altruistic soul,
who made a difference to so many.
Neil will remain in our hearts,
forever and always.

Never confined to a photograph,
nor consumed by time.
You will be in our thoughts,
until we can all meet again.

Restart your adventure

Wallowing in self-pity
hidden deep in a hole,
you are what you think you are
you pitiful soul.

If you allow fears to control you
you'll be too scared for life,
your thoughts will betray you
cutting you up from the inside.

Get your head up, be strong
give yourself time to shine,
beware the melancholy reaper
trying to monopolise your mind.

Show courage in adversity
take inspiration from others,
don't succumb to your anxieties
by hiding who you are under covers.

Some will want you to fail
some will give you their all,
find fortitude in belief
that you are not afraid to fall.

Drop the world from your shoulders
relinquish unrealistic control,
empower rational thinking
breathe deep and breathe slow.

Live life without excuses
be all you can be,
restart your adventure
set your tormented mind free.

Live forever

Lows of desperation mirroring the highs of love
are experiences we cannot escape,
unavoidable times
in the evolution of life,

losing the people we love is inevitable
enjoy every brief moment you have together,
appreciate your happiness
and hold onto it tight.

When we find ourselves consumed by loss
we can remember the sound of them laughing,
hear their voices
imagine their grins,

those sad times are a blessing
without them we would have never known love
and those everlasting feelings
love brings.

Happiness, it comes and goes
we marvel at its beauty
gradually take it for granted
and let it fade away,

melancholy times also come and go
often we tend to focus on them
they can take control
and maybe sometimes stay.

So hang on to your happiness
drink it up
rejoice in your chance
live without fear,

a smile, a flower, a friend, a lover
bathe in the beauty all around you
be content for when
the inevasible lows appear.

Make time for one more cuddle
find time to say I love you
cherish the time
we have together,

embrace your life
dare to smile
be true to yourself in knowing;
we simply can't all live forever.

You fill up my dreams

When I cannot protect you
from the toils of life
I will hold you in my arms
so we can just be alive.

Rising above all the turmoil
enjoying each moment we find
engrossed in our feelings
leaving the sad world behind.

Genuine serene smiles
not one of them a fake
every part of our love forges
the life that we make.

The look in your eyes
reveals my soul
I dote on your well-being
as one we are whole.

Averse to terse dramas
never enslaved by emotion
our love beautifully balanced
by our eternal devotion.

Tides of endearment
flood our existence
our hearts beat as one
without any resistance.

I miss you while I'm sleeping
at least that how it seems
as I close my eyes tightly
you fill up my dreams.

That one

The one for you
who you hold dear
makes you feel safe
when they are near,
who holds you tight
and shares your quarry
makes you feel safe
in times of worry.

The one for you
can show forgiveness
when all are raging
will share their kindness,
who offers hope
amid despair
wins you a teddy
at the fair.

The one for you
has fiery passion
shows empathy
defines compassion,
shares their warmth
when it is colder
holds your hand
as you get older.

The one for you
who gives you meaning
watches over you
while you are dreaming,
can make you tingle
with just a kiss
but when apart
the one you miss.

The one for you
who brings you laughter
fulfils a promise
of forever after,
a special one
who makes you whole
that one true love
will share your soul.

Inner child

My inculpable inner child
was wild
and carefree,

existing
without listening
to how others
would have me be.

Born to play
laughter filled my day
my strength was in my smile,

never giving in
from an origin of sin
struggling to find myself
going missing for a while.

Discontent at sharing
with the uncaring
I needed off this world,

then there was you,
you flipped my life in two
gave me a reason
my pathway unfurled.

From emotional purgatory
through life's magical observatory
my dreams so easy to see,

enthusiasm returned
a happiness I'd earned
forever grateful
someone so beautiful could ever love me.

Is love worth the pain

Darker times seem never ending
cruel emptiness devours our hearts,

jaded by negativity and regret
- is loving someone where the pain starts?

But without a chance
to love, are we;

simply blind to the beauty of life
and all that love can be?

So pull your loved ones in close
remind them that you care,

life enthused with hope
outweighs sorrow and despair.

Our empathy and kindness
can shine as brightly as the sun,

how much we share our hearts
defines who we become.

Convey your thoughts with passion
try to be forgiving,

embrace in the experiences of a life
you are fortunate to be living.

Because our eyes are filled
as time is billed,
with the souls of those who pass us by.

Time is yours

Distilled
with envy,
amid shadows
of eternal light,

resigned
to torment
prisoners
in nature's spite.

Plaintiffs of life
opportunist dreamers,
seeking happiness
we try;

to fill our days
though incomplete
alone,
beneath humble skies.

Surviving
waiting
looking for
a sign,

deluded
regretful,
as emphatic fools
of time.

To be me again

A harsh reality of life bestows us
the thoughts we have control us
over thinking,
imprisoned in our minds.

Irrationally perplexed
consumed by confusion
precious time lost,
a conjuring of delusion.

Mislead into panic
aboard a crazy train
terrified and ashamed,
of an invisible world of pain.

Desperate to avoid
an overwhelming fear
betrayed into belief,
the edge of sanity is near.

Searching for reason
amid irrational retort
to start enjoying my life,
instead of being controlled by thought.

To be me again
to smile and to laugh,
to have courage on my journey
as I try to find my path.

Out of sight

Into the ether, between dimensions I unravel.
Through fabric of space and of time I now travel.

Tormenting, bewildering, what journey am I on?
Confused, disorientated, just what have I become?

An agonising existence, of anguish, deceit.
Secluded vast plains, form a reluctant retreat.

Tumbled thoughts run amok, promoting magnificent contusion.
Unfamiliar reality, sparking inevitable delusion.

Emptiness engulfs me, a new feeling so strange.
My spirit floats alone, atop unwanted winds of change.

A freed soul without vessel, of undecided destiny.
I've not gone, you just can't see, my invisible entity.

Torn hearts, wounded minds, my loved one's shrouded in sorrow!
I see tears, I hear cries, I can't share their tomorrow.

They can't hear my shouts, they won't know my fate.
I'm marooned in isolation, in this catatonic state.

A guardian ever watching, a reliant seraph.
Seeing their sadness turn to smiles, as they reminisce and laugh.

Patiently waiting, hoping for our spirits to collide.
Dreaming of the embrace, that made us feel warm inside.

For a sparkle of hope, my presence, my light.
Deep down they know I've not left them, I am just out of sight.

The King

Fear not
we love you
a true God
of the game,

our love
will never cease
we will always
sing your name.

Majestic
audacity
a talisman
who marauders,

an enigmatic
intensity
for life
without borders.

Unashamedly
passionate
artistically
cavalier,

defiant of the
stereotype
your truth
c'est sincère.

Inspiring us
deeply
challenging
who we are,

philosophical
genius
you are The King;
Cantona!

There's no turning back

...the uncertainty of life
the certainty of friends you choose
the tragedies of the ones you lose
reflecting on those hours wasted.

Twisted concepts of declining hearts
empowering fears of dwindling passion
energy fuelled by love and laughter
carry us through the heart of the sun.

Unrelenting time cuts unforgiving deep scars
minds devoured, tormented to submission
our tired souls give out
but we never give in.

Desperately clinging to unaccomplished dreams
hollow remorse empty promise, distress,
with ability to adapt to chaos of change
responsibility outweighs our lustful desire.

Amidst desperate lows which consume us
we seek one more chance to glow
to re-live the moments that embossed our youth.
Relentless fools for eternity, pretending there's no end,

yet we never grow younger...

Hope

Happiness,
a state of being
is something I've come to know,
yet somehow
I've never felt,
as lonely
as how I feel
right now.

Hours
without conversation,
silence but for
background noises,
seemingly
on the brink of
despair,
deafened by irrational voices.

Undecided
how to move on,
or which way
to turn to,
frustrated
at my fall from
grace,
to some I'm just invisible.

Confused
by my own frailty,
knowing my thoughts
are all wrong,
questioning
my own self,
wondering
if I can stay strong.

Hope
is all I can have,
in moments
when I can't feel,
the love
for life around me,
and the worry
love is not real.

Our journey

As one we are us
harmonious together
for love is our glory,

with passion and verve
we seek out our dreams
we write our own story.

An enchanting romance
our smiles content
laughter is a feeling,

come rain or shine
as partners we dance
our lives have one meaning.

Genuine synchronicity
of pure electricity
as we realised we knew,

that tear in your eye
out of joy we both cried
as we both said "I love you".

Magical moments
fortify happiness
keeping our truth strong,

engrossed in our journey
day after day
simply living our love song.

On my own

Heavy hearted
forlorn regress
powerless to change
what cannot be undone,

a glass of nostalgia
less than half full
the bitterness of wasted time
yearning for that special someone.

A hollow emptiness
devours my inner self
consumed by guilt
as only I know,

memories of things
I never could do
of places where I
could never dare go.

No chances taken
shutting everyone out
my fears packed away
as if books on a shelf,

an existence simply
controlled by thought
restricted to reassuring routine,
yet completely safe from life itself.

Now is all there is

Now is all there is.
The past is behind us
each day a new adventure
today is yours;

yours to enjoy
to experience happiness
to be with your friends
who's joy you'll share,

cherish the time
you have with your loved ones
keep them in your thoughts
when they are no longer there.

Stay strong
be at peace
when others
raise their voices,

be positive
show courage
have confidence
in your own choices.

Have patience
be kind
wear your smile
from the inside,

embrace your day
be thankful
share your love
far and wide.

The ultimate feeling

A world of wonder surrounds us
a wealth of beauty
inspiration and intrigue,

a world brimmed with love and laughter
all we needed
was a chance to believe.

Love is our guide for togetherness
it defines who we are
and how we share,

sometimes overwhelmed by our meaning
yet the feelings we have
show we care.

Our thoughts can be as perfect
as a beautiful warm
summers day,

or sullen to depths of despair
as bitter as
the winter is grey.

With courage we can show our resilience
be brave and seek out
a kind shoulder,

being there for each other in all seasons
leaning in
each time it gets colder.

We can bask in our aura of kindness
to share in
a positive wellbeing,

as we searched for the answers to our lives
we discovered
our love is the ultimate feeling.

A shameful smile

A clandestine remark
from my mind as I embarked
on a downward turn,

instilled with regret
desperately trying to forget
the fears I've learned.

A brisk murmur of sort
empowered destructive thought
from truculent demons within,

reluctant truant from sanity
panic is normality
how I loathe its deplorable origin.

I wish for calmness
for someone to harness
the blight which consumes me,

spiraling helplessly
shaking incessantly
blinded by fears I cannot see.

I beg to ensconce
into thought nonchalance
to be void of all feeling,

an exhausting existence
draining all my resistance
for my mind I am pleading.

As if Jekyll and Hyde
uncontrollable inside
each day a new torment,

outside looking in
you just see a grin
as my shameful disguise for atonement.

Let me

Let me be your sparkle
let me be your guide
let me wear a proud smile
walking by your side.

Let me be your happy
let me be your friend
let me be your soul mate
who dotes on you no end.

Let me be your joker
let me be your clown
let me make you belly laugh
to chase away a frown.

Let me give you courage
let me be your shoulder
let us both hold hands together
even when we are much older.

Let me be your nuisance
let me be your lover
let me thank your depth of vision
to see past my outer cover.

Let me love you in the world
let us always be together
but mostly let me thank you for
the chance to share in your forever.

Good morning Princess

A constant celebration of our divine purpose
documenting our place within this ridiculous circus.

Your personal laureate words bring me to you,
you're all that I have, my dreams all come true.

I believe in the magic that we both share,
I believe our love carries us through testing times of despair.

The strength we have our souls in chorus,
ensure we hack out any storm laid before us.

I take pleasure as your jester my Kimberly May,
I enjoy being your respite on a weary day.

I'm embroiled in you and your beautiful smile
incoherent to all life's distractions so futile.

I lend to you my imagination and devout caring
to influence the positivity in the life we are sharing.

I know our memories will last a lifetime with others
but our moment is now, influencing as lovers.

Our passion, our laughter, our truth always told,
I bask in the safety of your hand that I hold.

My beautiful Princess who I truly adore,
day after day, I love you more and more.

The Whos

Existing
depicting
a subtle black abyss.
Glittering lights
glide as if by magic
illuminating darkness,
shimmering
as if subdued to dance,
sparkling jewels
glint proudly
within deep shadows
of perhaps a lucid umbrella.
A random trail
flashes mercilessly
across a sea of emptiness,
a moment of rebellion
betrayed to fall
from a disconsolate belfry,
a temporary slit
in the modest canopy
which contains us.
An infinite landscape
a vast corridor
of intrigue,
yet all within the bounds
of the tiniest speck of dust;
our world a mere droplet
upon a web of trivial deceit.

Your smile

A serendipitous relentless malaise
disobedient
thoughts filled the page,

incontinent questions of sanity
perhaps
they were my only normality.

A writing recluse on my lonesome
from
hero to zero, now no one,

a lost little boy without purpose
reluctant
to play in this circus.

Jilted by all rational ethos
spiralling
down into uncontrollable chaos,

once gluttonous with hope and proved glory
to
struggling to hold onto my story.

By chance given choice to regroup
to
spend my focus on doting on you,

life's passion returned now revealing
sharing
love is an actual meaning.

A Princess per se, avec savoir faire
your
light exorcised darkness and despair,

you reignited the warmth in my soul
prevented
past moments from taking their toll.

Our true destiny shared from the start
your
smile is what powers my heart,

my friend, my rock and devout guide
forever
my beautiful bride.

I don't actually know how I deserved to be with the most beautiful girl in the world

I try my best every day to make her smile

I can but love her forever,

and our love is the ultimate feeling.

The blurb

There's no denying the *GCSE Grade E which I earned in English wasn't one of my greatest achievements back in 1988. I was never academically gifted and despised school.

I sort of just started to write because it helped me process things which had happened in my life. This made me think more about my life, what was really important to me and how to deal with the unexpected. Hopefully some of it will help others learn from my experiences.

I also take great pride and enjoyment in expressing my love for Kimsy with the words I write. Kimsy is amazing, not only is she beautiful but she sees me for who I am and not what I look like, good job really!

My thoughts, (torn pages and all) are here for everyone to see. I'm always original and never ashamed...

(*I did manage a GCSE Grade D in French though, so maybe I should have written my thoughts in French).

Thank you for reading
and
sharing in my thoughts

Oggy
-x-

Printed in Poland
by Amazon Fulfillment
Poland Sp. z o.o., Wrocław